W9-AWT-060

Countries of the World

Argentina

Gareth Stevens Publishing
MILWAUKEE

About the Author: Nicole Frank is a graduate of Northwestern University. She has visited many countries and studied several languages. She now divides her time between writing and traveling.

PICTURE CREDITS
A.N.A. Press Agency: 14, 33 (top)
Giulio Andreini: cover, 33 (bottom), 46, 73, 87
Archive Photos: 10, 13, 15 (both), 29, 36 (top),
    50, 51, 74, 75, 79, 80, 81
Central Press Photos: 77
Sylvia Cordaiy Photo Library: 7
DDB Stock Photo: 39, 60
Focus Team: 2, 3 (top), 9 (top), 16, 18, 28,
    38 (both), 42, 62, 63, 66, 67, 68
Fox Photos: 52
Eduardo Gil: 1, 22, 70, 83
Michael Graber: 4
Blaine Harrington III: 43
HBL Network Photo Agency: 3 (bottom), 36
    (bottom), 37, 61, 64, 84, 85
Dave G. Houser Stock Photography: 23, 31
The Hutchison Library: 5, 6 (top), 21, 26, 32,
    49, 53, 59 (top), 82
Ministry of Tourism (Argentina): 71
North Wind Picture Archives: 69 (both)
Michael J. Pettypool: 17
Ira Rubin: 3 (center), 6 (bottom), 9 (bottom),
    35 (bottom), 59 (bottom), 56, 57
David Simson: 11, 20, 24, 25, 30, 33, 40, 41
    (bottom), 54 (both), 55, 76, 78, 89, 91
South American Pictures: 34, 35 (top), 41 (top),
    47, 48, 65, 72
Todo es historia: 44, 45
Trip Photographic Library: 8, 12, 27, 58
Rafael Wollmann: 19
Digital Scanning by Superskill Graphics Pte Ltd

Written by
NICOLE FRANK

Edited by
LEELA VENGADASALAM

Designed by
LYNN CHIN

Picture research by
SUSAN JANE MANUEL

First published in North America in 2000 by
Gareth Stevens Publishing
1555 North RiverCenter Drive, Suite 201
Milwaukee, Wisconsin 53212 USA

For a free color catalog describing
Gareth Stevens' list of high-quality books
and multimedia programs, call
1-800-542-2595 (USA) or
1-800-461-9120 (CANADA).
Gareth Stevens Publishing's
Fax: (414) 225-0377.

© **TIMES EDITIONS PTE LTD 2000**
Originated and designed by
Times Editions Pte Ltd
Times Centre, 1 New Industrial Road
Singapore 536196
http://www.timesone.com.sg/te

Library of Congress Cataloging-in-Publication Data
Frank, Nicole.
Argentina / by Nicole Frank.
p. cm. -- (Countries of the world)
Includes bibliographical references (p. 94) and index.
Summary: An overview of Argentina which provides information on
its geography, history, government, lifestyles, languages, art, food,
customs, and current issues.
ISBN 0-8368-2315-X (lib. bdg.)
1. Argentina -- Juvenile literature. [1. Argentina.] I. Series: Countries of
the world (Milwaukee, Wis.)
F2808.2.F73   2000
982 -- dc21   99-36635

Printed in Malaysia

1 2 3 4 5 6 7 8 9 04 03 02 01 00

Contents

AN OVERVIEW OF ARGENTINA

Argentina is the eighth largest country in the world and the second largest in South America after Brazil. A country of great beauty and diversity, Argentina's varied geography can be attributed to its incredible length — 2,300 miles (3,700 kilometers) in all! The climate is equally wide-ranging, from very hot in the north, near the Equator, to very cold in the south. The name *Argentina* means "silver," and early Spanish explorers came to the country to make a fortune from this precious ore. Although silver was never found in great quantities in Argentina, the name stayed. Argentina's capital is Buenos Aires, a cosmopolitan city that gives the country much of its pulse.

Opposite: **There are smiles all around as these men celebrate their climb to the top of Mount Fitzroy in Santa Cruz province.**

Below: **Buenos Aires is the largest and most populated of all the provinces in Argentina. It is the cultural and economic center of the country.**

THE FLAG OF ARGENTINA

The blue and white Argentine flag has an emblem in the center called the "Sun of May." According to legend, on May 25, 1810, while people were demonstrating against Spanish rule, the sun burst through the clouds in Buenos Aires, giving the crowds newfound hope. At about the same time, the demonstrators adopted the blue and white colors. Two years later, General Manuel Belgrano (1770–1820), leader of the independence movement, formed the triband flag of blue, white, and blue, which was later adopted as the national flag of Argentina. The color blue in the flag represents the midday sky in May, while the color white represents purity.

Geography

The Argentine Republic covers an area of nearly 1.1 million square miles (2.8 million square kilometers). It runs 2,300 miles (3,700 km) from north to south, stretching almost into Antarctica. Argentina is bordered by Bolivia and Paraguay to the north, Brazil and Uruguay to the northeast, and Chile and the Andes Mountains to the west. The Andes Mountains form a natural border between Chile and Argentina. Mount Aconcagua, at 22,834 feet (6,960 meters), is the highest peak in the Andes Mountains, as well as in the entire Western Hemisphere. Many people attempt to scale this peak every year, but few succeed. The Atlantic Ocean, which lies to the east, gives Argentina its vast coastline.

Geographical Zones

Argentina has four commonly recognized geographical zones: the pampas, the northeastern plains, Patagonia, and the Andes Mountains. The pampas, in central Argentina, cover a quarter of

IGUAZÚ FALLS

Iguazú Falls lies on the Iguazú River, which runs along the border between Argentina and Brazil. The thundering rapids are situated in a beautiful jungle setting.
(*A Closer Look, page 57*)

Left: **The Andes Mountains, which run the length of Argentina's western border with Chile, attract climbers from all over the world.**

Above: **The grasslands of the pampas cover much of the central region of Argentina.**

the country, and nearly 66 percent of the population lives there. Buenos Aires and several other large cities are located in this zone. Known for its fertile soil and grassy plains, the pampas can be divided into two regions: the dry pampas and the humid pampas. Cattle and agricultural industries are based in the pampas, making it an important economic area of Argentina.

The subtropical plains in the northeast are divided by the Paraná River into Mesopotamia and Argentina's share of the Gran Chaco region. Most of Argentina's wooded areas lie in these plains, including some lush tropical rain forests in Mesopotamia.

Southern Argentina is called Patagonia. Although it makes up 25 percent of the country, only 1 to 3 percent of the population lives there. Patagonia stretches all the way down to Tierra del Fuego, or "Land of Fire," an island at the tip of Argentina. The island got its name from early European explorers who saw it dotted with campfires.

The Andean highlands along Argentina's western border are home to some of the world's most rugged mountains, such as Mount Aconcagua.

NATIONAL PARKS

The nineteen national parks in Argentina are home to some of the country's untouched natural splendor. The glacier in Parque Nacional Perito Moreno, for instance, is getting bigger each year.
(A Closer Look, page 58)

Climate

Argentina lies in the Southern Hemisphere, so the seasons are opposite those in North America and Europe. Summer lasts from December through March, and winter from June through September. In the northeastern region, the winters are dry, while the summers are hot and humid. During these months, the temperature can go as high as 120° Fahrenheit (49° Celsius). Apart from the heat, this area experiences heavy rainfall. Traveling across the country from east to west, the yearly rainfall drops from an average of 60 inches (1,524 millimeters) to about 20 inches (508 mm).

The climate is mild in central Argentina. The pampas receive plenty of rain in the east but are fairly dry in the west. Because it sometimes gets very hot and humid in the summer months, many families in the Buenos Aires area leave for the beaches shortly after Christmas to escape the heat.

Patagonia, in the south, is the coldest part of Argentina. Some areas have moderate temperatures all year round due to the close proximity of the Atlantic Ocean. Farther south, however, it is both colder and windier. Eastern Patagonia is very dry, and there are stretches of desert in some areas due to the absence of rain.

Above: **Whale watchers get excited after spotting some whales in Península Valdés, which is off the coast of Chubut province.**

Plants and Animals

Argentina has a variety of habitats for plants and animals. There are rain forests in the north, pine forests on the Atlantic coast, and tropical jungles in Mesopotamia. The country has nineteen national parks, which are home to wild animals. The parks are also preserved as undeveloped areas to allow plants to thrive.

Argentina is home to the *quebracho* (kay-BRA-cho) tree. This tree, which grows in the Chaco region, is nicknamed the "axbreaker" because of its strong, hard wood. Quebracho is used to make telephone poles and railroad ties, and the acid from its bark is used to prepare leather.

There are a number of animals unique to Argentina. The rhea, for instance, is a large, three-toed bird that closely resembles an ostrich. It lives in the pampas and grows to a height of about 4 feet (1.2 m). Like ostriches, rheas cannot fly. The capybara, the world's largest rodent, also lives in Argentina and grows to about 4 feet. Its average weight of about 110 pounds (50 kilograms) is almost the weight of a pig! Herbivorous, the capybara eats plants by the water's edge, where it lives.

Above: **The rhea looks very much like an ostrich.**

Below: **Penguins live in colonies by the sea in southern Argentina.**

9

History

From the Colonial Period to Independence

The first settlers of South America began their journey in Asia in 24,000 B.C. They crossed the Bering Strait and made their way into North America. From there, they took thousands of years to travel through Central and South America. In 10,000 B.C, the first group of people reached Argentina, at the southern tip of South America.

In 1516, Juan Díaz de Solís, a Spanish explorer, arrived in Argentina. He was the first European to discover the area, but he and his men were soon killed by the Charrua tribesmen living there. Four years later, the Spanish explorer Ferdinand Magellan discovered the strait at the tip of Argentina that now bears his name. In 1526, Sebastian Cabot explored the Río de la Plata region and established the first settlement there, which was later abandoned. In 1536, another explorer, Pedro de Mendoza, arrived and founded the city of Buenos Aires.

Left: Sebastian Cabot sailed under the Spanish flag to Argentina. He was drawn by rumors of large deposits of silver in the country.

Left: **General José de San Martín (1778–1850) led the attack to rid South America of Spanish rule. He crossed the snowy Andes at Mendoza, with his troops, in twenty-one days. Once in Chile, he defeated the Spanish army at Chacabuco in 1817, and at Maipú in 1818. He then amassed a fleet of ships and sailed to Peru to force the Spaniards out of the country. In 1823, he returned to Argentina and retired from the army. In 1850, San Martín was elevated to the status of national hero. Statues of San Martín can be found in many Argentine cities.**

Permanently settling Argentina proved to be difficult. The native Indians, unhappy that settlers had come to their land, attacked them. It was only in 1580 that Buenos Aires became safe enough for settlers to reenter. During the second half of the sixteenth century, the new Spanish colonists set up small towns, such as Sante Fe and Córdoba. In the seventeenth century, they needed money and sold plots of land to private owners, which led to the creation of huge estates owned by Europeans and *criollos* (CREE-oh-yohs), people of European descent born in Latin America. In the latter half of the eighteenth century, the Spanish government that ruled Argentina faced financial difficulties and other problems. The British army took advantage of this situation to attack Buenos Aires. Two months after the attack, however, the townspeople drove the British troops out of the city. The British attacked and took the city again in 1807, but the townspeople persevered. On May 25, 1810, in what is known as The May Revolution, a new government was established in Buenos Aires. Six years later, on July 9, Argentina became officially independent. The next few decades, however, were marked by political turmoil in the country. In 1860, Argentina formally adopted its current name, and, two years later, Buenos Aires became the official capital.

The "Dirty War"

Upon Isabel's arrest, Argentina once again came under military rule. The military leaders began the "Dirty War." People suspected of "anti-government activities," as well as political leftists, were considered enemies. At least ten thousand people were killed or abducted in the night, never to be seen again. The military rule ended in 1983 with the election of Raúl Alfonsín as the first president of democratic Argentina, but, to this day, the mothers of those who disappeared demonstrate in the Plazo de Mayo every Thursday. They demand to know any information about their children who vanished some twenty years ago.

Above: **The Mothers of the Plaza de Mayo are a familiar sight every Thursday. They demand to know the whereabouts of their** *desaparecidos* **(des-a-par-eh-SEE-dos), or disappeared children, who have been missing since the "Dirty War."**

A Good Government

Carlos Saúl Menem was elected president as a candidate of the Peronist Party in 1989. Once he took office, he supported the need for freer markets and less government intervention. Menem has worked hard to control inflation and increase foreign investment in Argentina. Although not without problems, Menem's administration has seen considerable success.

Justo José de Urquiza (1801–1870)

Urquiza was responsible for drawing up the Argentine Constitution, which is still in use today despite some amendments. He modeled it after the U.S. Constitution. After it was adopted in 1853, Urquiza became president of Argentina. While in office, Urquiza's main focus was to unite the Argentine provinces. Although there was civil unrest during his rule, he was mostly successful in his aims. Apart from creating the Argentine Constitution, Urquiza negotiated a navigation treaty with the United States, Britain, and France. The treaty opened Argentine ports to international trade.

Juan Domingo Perón (1895–1974)

Juan Perón rose to political power in the 1940s as Minister of Labor. He was responsible for reforming Argentine labor laws. The changes were met with enthusiasm from the workers, and, in 1946, Juan Perón was elected president. Under Perón's rule, the masses enjoyed fewer rights, and the government took control of many industries, but the economy flourished. By Perón's second term, however, the country was facing extensive debts and high inflation. Perón fled to Spain in 1955, leaving Argentina nearly bankrupt. He returned in 1973 and was, once again, elected president.

Juan Domingo Perón

María Estela (Isabel) Martínez de Perón (1931–)

Isabel de Perón was Juan Perón's third wife. He married her while in exile in Spain. When Juan Perón returned to Argentina and became president in 1973, Isabel was appointed his vice-president. Upon the death of her husband in 1974, Isabel became president. She was the first woman ever to become president of a country in either of the Americas. Her presidency, however, was beset with problems. Argentina had long been suffering from a bad economy, and, while in office, Isabel saw inflation rise an astounding 400 percent! The country was also plagued by terrorism, which she was never able to root out. On March 24, 1976, Isabel Perón was arrested by the military and relieved of her power.

María Estela (Isabel) Martínez de Perón

Government and the Economy

Argentina has a republican, representative, federal system of government, which is divided into three branches: executive, legislative, and judicial. The head of the executive branch is the president, who is elected by the people to a four-year term. The president is also the head of the military. Serving directly under the president is the vice president.

The National Congress

The *Congreso Nacional*, or the National Congress, is made up of two houses, the Senate and the Chamber of Deputies. The Senate is led by the vice president and has forty-six members. Senators are elected by their local legislatures to six-year terms. The Chamber of Deputies has 257 members who are elected directly by the people. They serve four-year terms. Together,

THE FALKLAND ISLANDS/ISLAS MALVINAS

In 1592, English explorer John Davis sighted the Falkland Islands. The Argentine government claimed them in 1820, but the British ignored the claim. In 1833, the British took "formal" control of the islands.
(A Closer Look, page 52)

Below: The Congress building houses the Senate and the Chamber of Deputies.

these two houses make up the legislative branch of the Argentine government. The judicial is based loosely on the American and European systems. Judges and courts make up this branch, and it operates on both federal and local levels.

Argentina has twenty-three provinces and one Federal District (Buenos Aires). Each province elects its own governor and has its own system of courts.

People and Politics

On the whole, Argentines are very much involved in politics. The country's rapid succession of presidents and military leaders gives the topic special relevance, and people often discuss the outcome of certain political events at length. With different political parties to choose from, ranging from the far left (supporters of socialism) to the far right (supporters of capitalism), Argentines have several options when the time comes to cast their votes. Voting is taken very seriously in Argentina. Because it is mandatory for people between the ages of eighteen and seventy to vote, Argentines find it necessary to keep abreast of political developments.

Above: **Presidential guards in their striking uniforms patrol the Plaza de Mayo, the site of the Presidential Palace in Buenos Aires.**

TIERRA DEL FUEGO

Meaning "Land of Fire" in English, Tierra del Fuego is divided between Argentina and Chile. The Argentine section includes, among others, the cities of Ushuaia and Río Grande. Despite the island's lack of major attractions, increasing numbers of tourists are going there to soak up its natural beauty.
(*A Closer Look, page 68*)

Economy

Argentina has the highest per capita income in Latin America, and most Argentines enjoy a reasonable standard of living. In the past, however, Argentina's economy was marked by great instability. Among the wealthiest countries in the world in the early twentieth century, Argentina had become one of the poorest by the 1970s. High inflation and severe national debts, the effects of which can still be seen today, deeply scarred the country. It was only with the election of Carlos Saúl Menem as president, in 1989, that Argentina began to establish some level of economic stability. A proponent of fewer government restrictions, increased

privatization, and free trade, Menem has successfully led Argentina through tough economic times.

The Argentine economy, which was traditionally based on agriculture, is now expanding to include several different sectors. This diversification has helped the import/export market and has enabled Argentina to produce more varied goods, both for domestic consumption and for export to the rest of the world.

Above: **A worker sprays pesticide on a vegetable field. Argentina's agricultural crops significantly contribute to its economy.**

From Agriculture to Hydroelectric Power

Since the 1960s, Argentina has turned its attention away from the successful beef industry to agriculture. Today, the majority of Argentina's exports comes from the farming and food processing sectors. In fact, 12 percent of the country's land is used to grow crops.

Argentina's vast coastline serves as a base for a thriving fishing industry. More than 700,000 tons of fish are caught off the coast each year, and about 90 percent is shipped abroad, making an important contribution to the Argentine economy.

Argentina also has a wealth of natural resources spread across the country. In the foothills of the Andes Mountains, there are great deposits of minerals, gold, lithium, and copper. Oil and natural gas are also important to the Argentine economy. Nearly 70 percent of the country's energy comes from oil. Argentina

THE BEEF INDUSTRY

Most Argentines love to eat beef. They also export this meat overseas. The heart of Argentina's cattle industry is the pampas. It is believed that the grasses there give Argentine beef its special taste.
(*A Closer Look, page 46*)

produces so much oil that oil exports leaped an unbelievable 13 percent in 1993. With its current reserves, Argentina will have enough oil for the next ten years, and it also has more natural gas than oil — enough to last the next thirty years.

Hydroelectric power is gaining momentum in Argentina. With an established hydroelectric plant running in Yaciterá along the Paraná River, plans are underway to set up more plants. There are about ten rivers that could potentially be harnessed for hydroelectric power. The Argentine government predicts that, in the near future, dams will provide a considerable portion of the country's power supply.

Above: **Argentina produces vast amounts of oil for domestic consumption as well as for export.**

People and Lifestyle

About 36 million people live in Argentina today. Only two other South American countries, Brazil and Colombia, have larger populations. Because of its size, however, Argentina is one of the least densely populated countries on the continent.

A Land of Immigrants

One unique aspect of Argentina is that there are so many people of European descent — about 85 percent of them — it could be sometimes mistaken for a European country. Although the percentage of actual foreign-born people has decreased from 30 percent in 1914 to about 13 percent today, they still number more than 4.5 million. It is easy to see why Argentina is often called a "Nation of Immigrants."

Today's vast majority of Argentines with European ancestry has not always been the case. Argentina was home to many native Indians before the Spaniards colonized it. Most of these Indians, however, were killed during the period of colonization, and,

AFRO-ARGENTINES

Once a big part of Argentine society, Afro-Argentines have all but disappeared from Argentina today. How did they arrive in Argentina, and what are the reasons for their disappearance?
(A Closer Look, page 44)

Below: **Most Argentines have European ancestry.**

20

today, only 3 percent of the population is made up of indigenous people. They are found in the extreme northern and southern parts of the country.

City Folk versus Country Folk

Although there are several other large cities in Argentina, Buenos Aires is the only world-class city. It has a European flair and a cosmopolitan atmosphere. Just over twelve million people live in Buenos Aires and its suburbs. Argentines living here are called *porteños* (por-TAY-nyos), which means "people of the port." Porteños enjoy the wonderful arts scene, nightlife, and restaurants that contribute to city living. They are seen as sophisticated and cultured.

In contrast to the porteños are the country dwellers who inhabit the rest of Argentina, from Jujuy to Tierra del Fuego. They usually work in the agriculture, cattle, or manufacturing sectors. From the porteños' point of view, rural dwellers live a very sheltered life, not nearly as glamorous as their own. People living in the country, however, claim they are more environmentally conscious and down-to-earth than their counterparts from the city.

GAUCHOS

Gauchos are similar to the cowboys of the North American Wild West. Traditionally, they were known for their bravery and their ability to tame wild horses. Today, most gauchos work on sheep or cattle ranches and lead a quieter lifestyle.
(A Closer Look, page 54)

Family

Families are important and closely knit in Argentina. Often, grandparents, parents, and children all live in the same household, forging close relationships. While teenagers in other countries often leave home at eighteen to go to college, in Argentina, 69 percent of young adults between the ages of fourteen and twenty-nine live with their parents. They usually do not move out until they are married, and, even then, they live in a place near their family home.

Extended Family

The extended family plays a significant role in Argentine life. Aunts, uncles, cousins, grandparents, and even best friends remain close, meeting for family barbecues or picnics every few weeks. Cousins, who are often of the same age, become instant friends and trusted playmates, giving children an immediate circle of friends and tightening the bonds within families.

Below: **Parents try to spend as much time as possible with their children — both at home and outdoors.**

Argentina is a predominantly Roman Catholic society, where divorce has only recently been legalized. For a brief period during the 1950s, divorce was allowed, but it was quickly banned again. Today, when couples in Argentina divorce, children generally see both their parents and grandparents on a regular basis. Because couples involved in a divorce are concerned about their children's adjustment and well-being, they try to keep in touch with their in-laws even after their marriages break up.

Above: **In Argentina, a high premium is placed on women's looks. Rates of anorexia nervosa and bulimia are three times higher than those in the United States. Although many Argentine women are considered beautiful, a significant percentage of the female population undergoes plastic surgery to enhance their looks.**

The Role of Women

Throughout modern Argentine history, women have made giant leaps to better their position in society. Evita Perón, while first lady of Argentina, lobbied hard to increase women's rights in the workplace and, in 1947, helped women gain the right to vote. Isabel Perón, Juan Perón's third wife, also increased the visibility of women when she became the first female president in the Americas in 1974. The past sixteen years of democracy have further improved the state of women's rights. Today, 40 percent of the work force is made up of women, and a third of all households are partially supported by their incomes. While women still seem to be more respected at home than in the workplace, the situation is slowly changing.

Education

Argentina's literacy rate stands at an astonishing 96 percent, one of the highest in the world. The country is home to more than forty thousand educational institutions — schools, kindergartens, and universities. The educational system, however, has long suffered from a lack of government funding. In his last two terms in office, President Menem has tried to increase national funding for education.

The School System

About ten million people in Argentina attend schools, almost a third of the country's total population. Children complete seven years of compulsory primary education. If they wish to continue their education, they can go on to a secondary school and then to a university. Most students try to gain English proficiency while at school. The ability to speak and write English is considered a major asset in the business world.

Left: Argentines place great emphasis on education. Many try to gain entry into a university after their secondary education.

There are over fifty universities in Argentina, twenty-four of which are national universities funded by the government. One of these is the University of Buenos Aires. Founded 177 years ago, it is one of the oldest educational institutions in Argentina, and it has more than 170,000 students. This university, which has a strong tradition in science and technology, is the only one in Latin America to have produced three Nobel laureates from various scientific fields.

Above: **The University of Buenos Aires attracts many bright students each year.**

Health and Social Security

Argentina has one of the most advanced public health systems in Latin America. The system is jointly funded by the state and by private parties, and, with its extensive reach, makes itself accessible to most of the general population.

Argentina also has a system of social security. Each month, a portion of employees' salaries are withheld and added to the social security fund. This fund provides total health coverage. There is also a separate system of social security for self-employed or independent business persons.

Religion

Most Argentines are Roman Catholics. Ninety percent of the population declares Catholicism as its religion, although only 20 percent of this figure practices it regularly. Spanish colonial influence is responsible for the role of Catholicism in Argentine society today. For a long time, Argentine presidential candidates had to be Catholic. In 1994, when the constitution was revised, this law was dropped, and the president can now be of any faith.

The Virgin Mary

Every year, people journey to Luján, a small city just west of Buenos Aires, to worship the patron saint of Argentina, *La Virgen de Luján* (lah VEER-hen day loo-HAAN). According to one story, a statue of the Virgin Mary, which was being transported by wagon between churches, became stuck in the town of Luján, despite people's efforts to move it. Roman Catholics took this as a sign that the Virgin did not want her statue to leave the spot, so it remained in Luján. The statue now resides in its own chapel.

Each year, large groups make pilgrimages to Luján to pray to the Virgin. People come from all over the country to be part of this

Below: The church of San Francisco in Salta is believed to have the tallest tower in South America.

celebration. Many walk from Buenos Aires, 40 miles (64 km) away; others take the bus or travel by car. There is an open-air mass at the end of the journey, at which people pray and give thanks to the Virgin. Every year, an estimated 4 million people travel to see La Virgen de Luján.

Above: **A Sunday congregation makes its way to a local church.**

Judaism

Jewish people make up approximately 2 percent of the Argentine population — the largest Jewish community in Latin America.

Argentina's switch to democracy during the 1980s benefited the Jewish people there. The change helped them understand the local culture, and this eased their transition into Argentine society. In 1988, the Argentine Congress passed a law against anti-racism and anti-Semitism. Although the new law was an encouraging move, it did not totally eliminate some of the problems faced by Jewish people. In 1994, a bomb in a Buenos Aires Jewish community center killed over a hundred people. The Jewish community was outraged and demanded more government protection.

Language and Literature

Argentina's official language is Spanish, but it is different from the Castilian dialect spoken in Spain. There are many variations between the two in terms of pronunciation. Certain consonants, such as *ll*, are not pronounced with a "y" sound, as they are in Castilian Spanish, but rather as "sh" or a soft "j." Small, yet important, changes such as these give Argentine Spanish a style and sound all its own.

Apart from the Spanish dialects, other languages are also spoken in Argentina. English is the country's second language, and people living in large cities usually understand it. Lunfardo is a mix of languages that was developed at the end of the

Below: A "statue" reads a newspaper, as art imitates life.

nineteenth century around Buenos Aires. It is a combination of Italian, Portuguese, Spanish, French, German, and African words. Because Argentina has a large immigrant population, languages such as German, Italian, and French, are also prevalent. The country's rich cultural diversity is mirrored in the variety of languages and dialects spoken.

The Literary Scene
Argentina is home to many famous authors, including Adolfo Bioy Casares, Ernesto Sabato, and numerous others. The country's publishing business is a large and lucrative industry. Bookstores can be found on almost every street in the cities, and people are avid readers of books and newspapers. Literature is a successful and well regarded art in Argentina.

Above: **Jorge Luis Borges wrote books that made him popular all over the world.**

Victoria Ocampo
Victoria Ocampo was an aristocratic writer who had a profound influence on Argentine literature during the early twentieth century. She started a literary magazine called *Sur* in 1931. It published the works of Argentine writers and was a huge success, with an international circulation.

Jorge Luis Borges and Manuel Puig
One of the authors featured in Ocampo's magazine was Jorge Luis Borges. Borges is the most famous and influential writer in Argentina's history. He was born in Buenos Aires in 1899 and gained recognition as part of the city's avant-garde during the 1920s. He is widely regarded as a poet, although he also wrote essays, short stories, and prologues. His books, which include *Ficciones* (Fictions, 1944), *El Aleph* (1949), and *Otras Inquisiciones* (Other Inquisitions, 1952), have all been successful, winning him fans and praise both within Argentina and around the world. Borges was nominated several times for the prestigious Nobel Prize for Literature, although he never won it. He died in 1986.

Another influential Argentine writer was Manuel Puig. He wrote the international bestseller *Kiss of the Spider Woman*, which was translated from a book to a play and staged around the world. Puig was a writer of exceptional quality, known for weaving interesting stories into sophisticated formats. Despite the complexity of his stories, however, they were easily understood.

THE PROBLEM OF EXTINCTION

One problem facing Argentina is the extinction of its native languages. As the native people of Argentina slowly die off or intermarry, their languages, too, are disappearing. Indian tribes are losing numbers quickly, and linguists fear the day when no one is left to keep these languages alive.

Arts

Buenos Aires: The Paris of Latin America

Argentina has always had a varied arts community, representing many different art forms and styles. Through the country's turbulent political periods, however, art suffered. The government banned some artists and their works. Today, Buenos Aires is the center of the art world in Argentina. This city, which prides itself on being "The Paris of Latin America," reflects great European influences and techniques in its art. The city hosts a number of museums that display Argentine art, most notably the National Fine Arts Museum.

Works in Silver

When Spanish explorers arrived in Argentina, they thought the land was rich in silver. The abundance of silver, however, proved to be a rumor. The first silversmiths came to the country during the eighteenth century. Like many people during that time, they were immigrants from Europe and settled in Buenos Aires.

BUENOS AIRES: THE HEART OF ARGENTINA

Buenos Aires, the last major city to be founded in Latin America, is now a vibrant, cosmopolitan area. It is where most of the action in Argentina takes place, from cultural events to weekly demonstrations.
(*A Closer Look*, page 48)

Below: **A street performer wows crowds with his daredevil antics.**

Above: **A makeshift store selling silverware and other items attracts the attention of passersby.**

Although silver is not found in large quantities in Argentina, beautiful silver work can be found across the country. The gauchos of the pampas have always used a lot of silver to make the tools of their trade. Spurs for their boots, bridles for their horses, and stirrups for their saddles are all made out of silver. In addition, the mate gourd and the *bombilla* (bom-BEE-zha), or long straw, used to drink *yerba mate* (YAIR-ba MAH-tay) are often made of delicate and intricate silver work. Some of these silverware items can be found in museums, where they are part of permanent displays.

Silver work has also been important in the decoration of Catholic churches. Silversmiths used Catholic images and native detailing in their work. Their masterpieces adorned the churches during the colonial period. Unfortunately, around this time, most of the art work was stolen from Argentina, during its wars with Portugal. Silver work was popular during Argentina's struggle for independence, and it has always held a small niche in the art world, but it was not until the 1960s that it made a comeback.

TEATRO COLÓN

Teatro Colón attracts some of the best singers in the world. Nearly two hundred years old, this opera house in Buenos Aires is a mix of different architectural styles.
(A Closer Look, page 66)

Painting

In its early history, as more and more people settled in Argentina, demand increased for more art and artists. Initially, the wealthy bought paintings in Europe and sent them to Argentina. Later, they got painters to come to Argentina to paint the scenes of their new country. Buenos Aires became the center of the painting world, and, slowly, Argentine artists began to emerge.

Italian Carlos Enrique Pellegrini was a famous foreign artist who came to Argentina to paint portraits of the wealthy. His works can still be found in the National Fine Arts Museum. Prilidiano Pueyrredón is widely recognized as Argentina's first national painter. He painted landscapes and portraits and became famous during the mid-nineteenth century.

The World of Movies

The Argentine movie industry did not start until the end of World War I, twenty years after the European and North American industries. By the 1930s and 1940s, going to the movies was a very popular leisure activity in Argentina. There were over

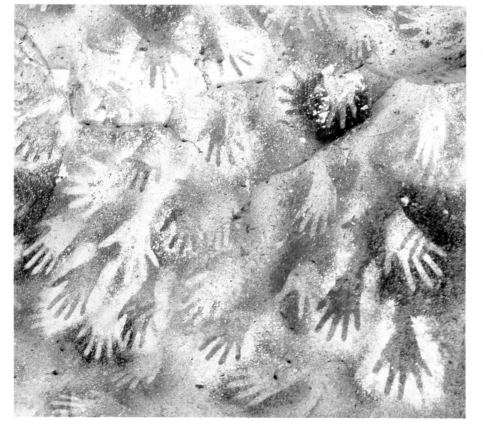

Left: This 2,000-year-old painting can be found in the Cave of the Painted Hands in Santa Cruz province.

1,500 cinemas in the country. Despite all these venues, however, the majority of movies shown were made in the United States and Europe. The Argentine movie industry began to prosper only in the later half of the twentieth century.

In the 1930s, Carlos Gardel, Argentina's most famous tango singer, starred in Hollywood movies. Hollywood used Gardel to attract more Hispanic viewers to the movies. Gardel's films were successful, but a fatal plane crash in 1935 abruptly ended his movie career.

Stops and Starts

When the military junta took control of Argentina's government in 1976, the movie industry suffered. The government placed strict regulations on movies. Not until 1983, when democracy returned to Argentina, did the situation take a turn for the better. The best-known movies made during the 1980s and 1990s dealt with very serious topics, such as "The Dirty War." *The Official Story* by Luis Puenzo, *Buenos Aires Viceversa* by Alejandro Agresti, and *The Night of the Pencils* by Hector Olivera all focused on war and the people affected by it. In 1986, *The Official Story* won an Academy Award for Best Foreign Language Film.

THE TANGO

The dance most often associated with Argentina, the tango, is now popular all over the world. Although not accepted by society in the early 1900s, by 1915 it had become the rage in European circles.

(*A Closer Look*, page 64)

Leisure and Festivals

The larger cities in Argentina offer a variety of leisure activities. Buenos Aires has extensive shopping, which keeps many people busy on weekends. Buying the latest fashions or scouring the shops for great bargains are always popular pastimes. Argentines are also avid players and fans of sports. *Fútbol* (FOOT-ball) is a national craze, and the country is renowned for its polo players. All over Argentina, eating out is a common way to spend late evenings with family and friends. These activities, together with the cultural events that take place every night, make Argentina a great place to relax and have fun.

Confiterías

Sitting in a café, or *confitería* (con-fit-a-REE-a), and watching the world go by is a favorite pastime among people in Buenos Aires. People read the paper or play a game of chess or dominos, as they sip a cup of coffee or a cold drink. Confiterías are the center of

TRAIN TO THE CLOUDS

A train in Salta takes passengers to dizzying heights as it makes its way between Salta and Chile. Along the journey, passengers can take in the beautiful scenery of Argentina.

(A Closer Look, page 70)

Below: **Argentines love to relax with friends in outdoor cafés.**

social life in the city. People often meet at a favorite confitería before an evening out or after a night on the town. These cafés are located all over the city. Every confitería has a signature style. Some are known for their intense political discussions, others as student hangouts, and still others for their fine pastries. While confiterías are popular places to meet people and relax, they are also places to be alone. A confitería is a great place to enjoy your solitude and collect your thoughts.

Beaches

During the summer months of January and February, Mar del Plata and its surrounding area become the most popular spots in Argentina. The seaside town of Mar del Plata began to flourish during the 1930s, and it has not looked back since. Every year, thousands of people from Buenos Aires flock to this resort area to enjoy the beaches and nightlife. Several newer resorts have appeared along the coast, which is just a four-hour drive from Buenos Aires. People enjoy fishing, golfing, horseback riding, sunbathing, gambling, and eating out. Other towns along the coast, such as San Bernardo, Pinamar, and Villa Gessell, are also crowded during the summer months.

Sports

When it comes to sports, Argentines are an active bunch. Although best known for their soccer and polo players, many other sports are played across the country. Argentina's varied climate and topography lends itself well to a wide range of athletic endeavors.

Snow sports are popular in Argentina. The Andes are a hot spot for adventurous climbers, and people travel from all over the world to scale the Aconcagua peak. There are ten routes to the top, but ascent is still a challenge. Skiing is also a favorite pastime. The season usually starts in May and ends in October.

Tennis Aces

Tennis gained enormous popularity in the 1970s and 1980s, with the emergence of Argentine stars Guillermo Vilas and Gabriela Sabatini. These two players catapulted to the top of the rankings, and, soon, most of Argentina was following their lead to play tennis, either competitively or for recreation. Rugby, golf, auto racing, and boxing are other sports that have found enthusiastic participants and spectators in recent years.

Above: Gabriela Sabatini increased the profile of tennis in Argentina.

Below: The ski resorts at Bariloche (in Río Negro province) and Las Leñas (in Mendoza province) are popular with both Argentines and tourists.

Fútbol Fever

Soccer, or fútbol, was introduced to Argentina during the 1800s, when the British brought the game to South America. The sport grew in appeal and is now a phenomenon in the country. Argentina's national team has won the World Cup Championship twice, in 1978 and again in 1986. In addition to their national team, Argentina has several professional teams. The two most popular soccer teams are Boca Juniors and River Plate, both from Buenos Aires.

People are obsessed with soccer and its players. The most famous player in Argentina's soccer history is Diego Maradona, who had an incredible career as a soccer player in South America and Europe. He is best known for the controversial goal he scored in the 1986 World Cup finals. His goal led to Argentina's victory over England and earned Maradona the Best Player title for the entire tournament. In 1994, Maradona was suspended from playing soccer, for a second time, when he tested positive for drugs at the World Cup. Although he staged a comeback in 1996, he has since retired.

Above: **Diego Maradona (*center*) is considered the best soccer player to come out of Argentina. Some believe that he was the best soccer player in the world at the peak of his career.**

POLO

This game played on horseback was brought to Argentina by the British and has since flourished in the country. Top polo players earn huge incomes and travel around the world to take part in prestigious polo competitions.
(A Closer Look, page 60)

Festivals

Argentina's lively regional festivals attract many tourists. Some of these celebrations even draw Argentines from all over the country. The Alpine Chocolate Festival in the small village of Villa General Belgrano; the Gaucho Festival, or Tradition Week, in San Antonio de Areco; and the Fiesta del Poncho in Catamarca are some examples of exciting annual celebrations.

Above: Children have fun during Carnival in loud, funny costumes.

Carnival

Although the Carnival celebrations in Argentina are not as big as those in Brazil, the northern part of the country still joins in the festivities. Carnival is one of the Roman Catholic celebrations that take place around the world. It begins on the Friday before Ash Wednesday, usually in February. People dress in colorful and elaborate costumes, and parades are held in the streets. Cities on the northern border of Argentina near Bolivia, such as Humahuaca and Tilcara, celebrate Carnival with the most enthusiasm. In Tilcara, flowered statues representing the Stations of the Cross are on display, while processions fill the streets on Ash Wednesday.

Below: A woman dressed in an elaborate outfit enchants the crowds in the streets during Carnival.

Wine Festival

Vendimia (ven-dee-MEE-a) is held every year in the city of Mendoza. This week-long festival takes place in March and honors the ripening and harvesting of wine grapes. There are folk concerts and events throughout the week, and tens of thousands of visitors arrive to take part in the celebrations. People dance and drink in honor of their provinces and in appreciation of their hard work. Each year, a bishop blesses the wine, and there is a large parade with local bands, numerous floats, and antique cars. The celebration comes to an end with the crowning of the Wine Harvest Queen and a spectacular fireworks display.

Folk Music and Dancing Festival

The National Folklore Festival takes place in Cosquin in the province of Córdoba. Cosquin has been dubbed the "National Folklore Capital," and, every year, during the last week of January, hundreds of people come to celebrate folk music and folk dancing. Although the village holds many festivals throughout the year, this one is the most important and well known.

Below: **Men and women perform a dance as part of the Gaucho National Festival, which takes place during the summer.**

Food

Authentic Argentine cuisine exists only in small pockets across the country. Most of the food eaten in Argentina has been adapted from other cultures, especially European. Spanish, Italian, and German foods have all had an influence. Although their native dishes may number few, Argentines love to eat out. Restaurants dot the cities, staying open late to accommodate their patrons.

Breakfast is not a big meal in Argentina. People usually eat something light to tide them over, then have lunch some time after noon. Late afternoon is a popular time for people to go out for a small snack or some pastry. Dinner is the biggest meal of the day. It is served late at night, sometimes lasting until after midnight. Restaurants are often open long into the night.

If there is one staple in the Argentine diet, it has to be beef. The cattle industry is huge in Argentina and accounts for about 5 percent of the country's exports. The Argentine people love meat and eat it at least once a day. In addition to beef, Argentina also makes excellent wines, with the red wines being better than the whites. The country has had wineries since 1554 and consumes most of its own product.

Below: **Argentina is the fifth-largest wine producer of the world. Most Argentines have wine with their meals.**

Left: **A barbecue is often the occasion for getting together with friends and enjoying different types of meat.**

Popular Dishes

Parrilla (par-REE-zah) is a dish many Argentines enjoy. It is Argentina's version of the American barbecue, where meat is roasted on a grill over hot coals. This dish is a mix of different meats and cuts, sometimes including udders, intestines, and kidneys, along with more traditional cuts. Parrilla is a big meal, and several people eat from the same dish. Another interesting way of serving meat is called *asado* (ah-SAH-do). Asado refers to the way meat is grilled, on a spit over hot coals. This method of cooking was popularized by the gauchos of the pampas.

Other popular dishes in the country include *chorizos* (cho-REE-sos), or spicy sausages; *empanadas* (aym-pah-NAH-dahs), or pastries stuffed with meat, vegetables, or cheese; *ensalada mixta* (en-sah-LAH-thuh MEEKS-ta), or lettuce with tomatoes, onions, oil, and vinegar; and *locro* (LOH-kroh), a hearty corn-based stew.

YERBA MATE

A unique Argentine beverage, mate is a type of tea that can be enjoyed any time of the day. It is believed to have special curative powers.

(A Closer Look, page 72)

A CLOSER LOOK AT ARGENTINA

This section describes the sights and sounds of Argentina that make the country unique. Buenos Aires, Argentina's capital, bustles with cultural events and a roaring nightlife. In contrast, Tierra del Fuego, an island found at the tip of Argentina, is home to some beautiful scenery and quiet Ushuaia, the southernmost city in the world.

There are many places for the adventurous to explore in Argentina. The Train to the Clouds takes you on an unforgettable trip through the Andes at unbelievable heights. In northeastern Argentina, Iguazú Falls delights and amazes tourists from around the world.

Argentina is also known for the sultry tango. This dance has been a symbol of Argentine life for decades. Small tango clubs dot the city of Buenos Aires, and, as people perform the sophisticated moves, it is easy to see why the tango is one of the most popular dances in the world.

Opposite: **Soccer matches attract capacity crowds in Argentina — a soccer-crazy country like its neighbor Brazil.**

Below: **Music is part of most celebrations in Argentina. Fairs dedicated exclusively to music, for instance, are a good way of understanding Argentines' passion for the arts.**

43

Afro-Argentines

The Afro-Argentines, who made up a large percentage of the population through the 1700s and early 1800s, had virtually disappeared by the end of the nineteenth century. Today, they account for a very small percentage of the population. The mystery of their disappearance continues to intrigue historians and sociologists.

In the sixteenth century, Spaniards brought black Africans into Argentina to work as slaves. By 1778, 30 percent of the population of Buenos Aires was Afro-Argentine. The slaves encountered many problems — living and working conditions were miserable, and they were treated poorly. In 1813, the slave trade was outlawed, but the ban did little for Afro-Argentines already enslaved. Many of them were recruited, a few years later, to fight the Spaniards during the war for independence. The government bought slaves from their owners and enlisted them

Below: **Although Argentina is now predominantly a European society, Afro-Argentines once formed a large percentage of the population.**

44

in the army, with the promise that they would be freed in five years' time if they survived. Ironically, hundreds of slaves fought for the country's independence, although they themselves were not free people. By 1827, most slaves were freed by their owners, but, for some, freedom did not come until decades later. Slavery was finally abolished in Argentina in 1853. Over the years, the percentage of Afro-Argentines dropped dramatically. In 1836, they made up 26 percent of the population in Buenos Aires, but in 1887, only 1.8 percent.

There are several theories to explain the puzzle of the Afro-Argentines' disappearance, although no theory has ever been proven. George Reid Andrews researched the topic in depth and wrote a book called *The Afro-Argentines of Buenos Aires 1800–1900*. He has four theories that might explain the fate of these people.

First, he proposes that the yellow fever epidemic of 1871 could have devastated the population. Second, the population could have diminished when Afro-Argentines were freed and began intermarrying with whites, thus lowering the number of racially pure blacks in the country. Andrews also theorizes that warfare had a negative effect on the population. Finally, he proposes that because slavery was eventually abolished, no new slaves were brought into the country to increase the numbers of Afro-Argentines already there.

The Beef Industry

Beef: The King of Meats

Beef has been a staple of the Argentine diet for hundreds of years and continues to hold an important place in the culture, cuisine, and economy of the country.

Although now abundant there, cattle are not indigenous to Argentina. The first livestock came to the country from Spain in 1556. With its temperate climate and extensive grasslands for grazing, Argentina proved a suitable setting for raising cattle.

Originally, there were more cattle than the country could use, but, by 1810, the first salting plants were opened, so beef could be dried and preserved. By 1882, Argentines made use of the process of refrigeration and would soon ship beef on refrigerated boats bound for Europe. Since the late 1800s, Argentina's international market for beef has increased tremendously. It now exports beef to over one hundred countries.

Below: Argentina has about 54 million head of cattle, which means there are more cattle than people in the country.

Land to Graze

About 52 percent of Argentina's land is used for meadows and pastures. Each head of cattle has about 100 square miles (259 square km) of land to graze. Because land is plentiful, the cattle do not have to eat feed. Their diet consists of the grasses of the pampas. Many say this diet contributes to the special tenderness of Argentine beef. The warm climate allows cattle to graze all year round on the open plains.

Above: **Argentina is known for its high-quality, tender beef, considered one of the best in the world. Eating beef is a way of life in the country. The gauchos of the pampas also raise cattle for sport.**

For All Meals

Argentine people eat beef at almost every meal. The meat is widely available and affordable, and each Argentine is said to consume an average of 154 pounds (70 kg) of beef yearly. There are many different ways to serve beef, so the average diner does not get bored with it. It can be barbecued, boiled, grilled, fried, or made into sausages. Probably the most popular way to serve beef is with French fries, a salad, and a local red wine. Recently, as a result of warnings by health experts that an excess of red meat is bad for health, beef consumption has seen a decrease. Beef, however, is still preferred over other types of meats.

Buenos Aires: The Heart of Argentina

Buenos Aires ("fair winds" in English) was founded in 1536 by Pedro de Mendoza, a Spanish nobleman. The city was rather insignificant during the initial colonial period, but, in 1776, it became the capital of a new vice-royalty of Rio de la Plata, which stretched from modern-day Bolivia to Paraguay and Uruguay. During this time, the city's economy, based mostly on illegal trade, flourished. In 1862, after Argentina declared its independence and problems were resolved between the city and the other provinces, Buenos Aires was declared the country's capital. Soon after, it was named a Federal District and became the seat of government. In the early 1900s, Buenos Aires became an important port. Thousands of immigrants flocked to the city, and it subsequently became a cultural center for the country. By the mid-1900s, however, economic and political problems plagued it. Buenos Aires along with most of Argentina, was on a downward spiral.

Below: **Buenos Aires has often been called the most important city in South America. Although Buenos Aires has had a long and tumultuous history, it remains a cultural hub of the world.**

What Makes the City Tick?

Today, Buenos Aires is home to the Teatro Colón, the National Library, the Fine Arts Museum, Casa Rosada, and Catedral Metropolitana. Hundreds of bars, discotheques, restaurants, shops, and cafés can be found across the city.

The World's Widest Street

Avenida 9 de Julio in the downtown area of Buenos Aires is the widest street in the world, with a breadth of 460 feet (140 m). Many houses had to be demolished to accommodate the street's construction in the 1930s. The city center is called the Plaza de Mayo, where many demonstrations have taken place over the years. In the 1940s, Evita Perón led a demonstration to free Juan Perón; during the Falklands War, people initially came to cheer on their president, and, later, upon learning he had lied about winning the war, they demonstrated again. When Argentina won the World Cup for soccer in 1986, people gathered at the Plaza de Mayo to celebrate.

Above: The central pyramid of the Plaza de Mayo was built on the first centennial anniversary of Buenos Aires' independence.

Evita

A Fairy Tale Comes True

Evita was born in the poor village of Los Toldos, Argentina. From a young age, Evita, which means "little Eva," was determined to leave her poor surroundings and become an actress. Although this was a seemingly impossible wish, she was given a chance to move to Buenos Aires at the age of fourteen, and she took it. After a shaky start to her career, Evita finally earned a break when she was given her own radio show. She became a regular on the radio, and, through her job and her enthusiasm, she met several powerful people.

Meeting Juan Perón

Through these influential connections, Evita met Colonel Juan Perón, who was a respected figure in the new military

Left: **Evita's elegant clothes, jewelry, and glamorous lifestyle were admired throughout Argentina and the world. People were intrigued by Evita's life story — her poor childhood and her rise to fame.**

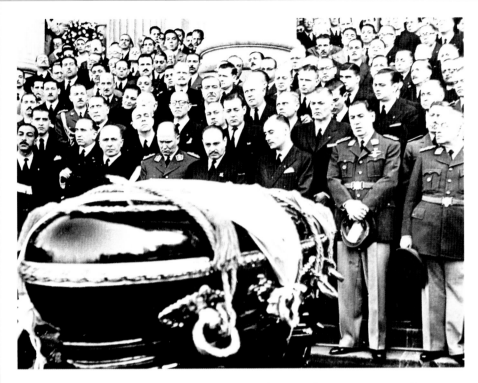

Left: At Evita's wake, thousands came to mourn her death. Evita's body now rests in Recoleta Cemetery, and her gravestone reads, "Don't cry for me Argentina, I remain quite near to you." Although she has been dead for almost fifty years now, people still leave flowers at her grave. Attempts to make Evita a saint, however, have failed.

government. Perón began a relationship with Evita, and when Perón became the Minister of Labor and Welfare, Evita was by his side. She is said to have given him the invaluable advice that would mark his career — to recognize the power base that existed among the thousands of poor villagers surrounding the city of Buenos Aires. Perón established a minimum wage, offered better living conditions, and increased the salaries of the labor force. He became a huge success with the masses. He married Evita in 1945 and became president of Argentina the following year.

Rising in Stature

As Perón rose to power, Evita's popularity also grew. Once Juan Perón was president, Evita established the Eva Perón Foundation, which built hundreds of hospitals, schools, and other charitable organizations. She also formed the Peronista Feminist Party in 1949, the first women's political party in Argentina.

In 1952, Evita died of cancer at the age of thirty-three. On July 26, the day of her death, Argentina was in shock. Evita's body was embalmed for preservation. After Juan Perón's death in 1974, her body was flown from Spain to Argentina, where she was laid to rest beside her husband. Even after her death, the Argentine people's fascination with her continued.

The Falkland Islands/ Islas Malvinas

Dispute over Claim

The Falkland Islands, known as the Islas Malvinas in Argentina, are an archipelago about 300 miles (483 km) off the eastern coast of Argentina in the south Atlantic ocean. The islands' economy centers on sheep farming. Although seemingly insignificant, this group of islands has been the focus of conflicting Argentine and British interests since the nineteenth century.

In 1982, a military junta was in control of the Argentine government, and army general Leopoldo Galtieri was president. The country was politically unstable. Foreign debt soared to billions of dollars, inflation was high, and unemployment left much of the population in poverty. Galtieri felt Argentines needed a diversion from domestic problems, so he turned their attention to the Falkland Islands.

Below: **The Falkland Islands have always been claimed by both Argentina and Great Britain. In 1833, Britain took control of the islands, despite Argentina's claim over them. Since then, the British have inhabited the islands and have stationed troops there.**

On April 2, 1982, Argentina invaded the Falkland Islands, determined to retake them from the British. Argentina's troops, however, were poorly trained and no match for the military might of Britain. Galtieri had underestimated Britain's defense of the islands; the British were determined to keep control. Although things were going badly for the Argentine military, Galtieri lied to the people of Argentina, telling them they were winning the war.

The war lasted seventy-two days, and over two thousand people were killed. Argentina lost its only cruiser, *General Belgrano*, when it was sunk by a British submarine on May 2. On June 14, 1982, Argentina surrendered but did not give up its claim to the islands. Argentines were devastated and outraged to learn that Galtieri had been lying to them about the country's victory. He resigned from office a few days after the end of the war.

The Falklands War had a great impact on Argentine history. It took seven years after the end of the war for Britain and Argentina to reestablish relations. In 1997, for the first time since the war, a small group of Argentines were allowed to visit the islands. Britain still has about two thousand troops protecting the Falklands.

Above: Recently, the Falkland Islands have begun to prosper. The fishing industry has become big business, and oil drilling is expected to begin within the next few years. Although the islands are 8,000 miles (12,872 km) away from Britain, the British government has no intention of giving them up.

Gauchos

Gauchos have long been seen as true symbols of Argentine culture. These horsemen of the pampas have been around for hundreds of years and have played an important role in Argentina's history. Some people argue that the authentic gaucho is a thing of the past; others disagree. Regardless of this debate, many Argentine horsemen today still call themselves gauchos.

The first gauchos in Argentina roamed the grasslands of the pampas as far back as the eighteenth century. They tamed wild horses and would round up wild cattle and kill them. Although they had no way to store or preserve the beef, the animal hides provided valuable income for the gauchos. They would sell the hides in exchange for goods.

During the late eighteenth century, the government gave large tracts of land to rich, powerful men, driving the gauchos out of the lands they once occupied and further away from the cities. As a result, the gauchos became isolated from society. Over time, they began to work as farmhands on large expanses of land

Above and *below:*
Taming a horse or a bull is a skill gauchos pick up at a young age.

54

Left: **A gaucho shows off his belt with its intricate silver buckle.**

called *estancias* (es-TAN-see-uhs). Today, gauchos can be seen on many of the estancias operating in Argentina. Estancias can be cattle ranches, sheep farms, plantations, agricultural farms, or large country houses and estates. Some even have their own vineyards for producing wine. Tourists are now welcome to visit and stay at many of these ranches and estates. These visits are valuable cultural experiences for the tourists and provide additional income for the owners.

Dressing Up

Gauchos wear *bombachas* (bom-BA-chas), which are loose pants comfortable enough for a day of riding. Around the waist, they wear a belt with a large, silver buckle. They also wear a *poncho* (PAWN-cho), a cape-like coat that keeps them warm at night. Most gauchos sport a kerchief around their necks, spurs on their boots, and a wide-brimmed hat to keep the sun out of their eyes. They also carry weapons, such as knives or *boleadoras* (bow-lee-a-DOOR-ahs). Boleadoras are made of three round stones on a leather strap. Used for hunting, they are thrown around the legs of animals to capture them.

Iguazú Falls

The Mighty Waters

Located on the Argentina/Brazil border, Iguazú Falls is a breathtaking spectacle. The falls were originally discovered in 1541 by Spanish explorer Alvar Núñez Cabeza de Vaca. They were forgotten, however, until a Brazilian expedition rediscovered them in 1863.

Iguazú Falls is located in the Misiones province of northeastern Mesopotamia, where the Iguazú and Paraná rivers converge. As the Iguazú River flows, it collects water from about thirty other rivers, increasing both the volume and force of the water. There are dangerous rapids above the falls, before the water drops some 270 feet (82 m). An enormous cloud of mist always hangs over Iguazú Falls.

Devil's Throat

Iguazú Falls is higher than U.S.-Canadian Niagara Falls and is one-and-a-half times as wide. It is actually 275 different waterfalls, the largest and most spectacular of which is Garganta del Diablo, or Devil's Throat. This waterfall drops more than 350 feet (107 m). Visitors used to be able to walk down to Garganta del Diablo on boardwalks, but severe floods in 1986 damaged them. Now, visitors view Devil's Throat from a boat, instead.

A Shared Attraction

Because Iguazú Falls lies on the border of Argentina and Brazil, the countries share the attraction. Most of the falls are in Argentina, but, the views are generally better from Brazil. The falls are surrounded by tropical jungle, and each country has established a national park bordering them to ensure the preservation of the area. The thick jungle provides a natural habitat for hundreds of birds, animals, and insects. Pumas, toucans, jaguars, and anteaters all can be found there.

The beauty of Iguazú Falls has attracted even the attention of Hollywood. The movie *The Mission*, which tells the story of Jesuit priests in South America during colonial times, was filmed there. This movie won the 1986 Cannes Film Festival Best Picture award as well as a 1987 Oscar for Best Cinematography.

Above: **The rare beauty of Iguazú Falls made it a World Heritage National Monument in 1984.**

Opposite: **The waters of Iguazú Falls are extremely powerful. Over the course of 130 million years, the falls have eroded a canyon 37 miles (60 km) long.**

National Parks

For a Green Environment

Argentina has an extensive national parks system to preserve the millions of acres of land that make up the country. There are nineteen national parks, some to protect endangered animals, some to preserve trees, and others to serve as nesting grounds, with one common aim — to conserve the land and protect the environment. In addition to the national parks, the country also has several national monuments, national reserves, provincial parks, and provincial reserves.

Argentina's first national park, Parque Nacional Nahuel Huapi, was established in 1934. Francisco Moreno, an Argentine who had explored Patagonia, was given a tract of land as a gift from the government for his work. Moreno handed the land back

Left: **Parque Nacional Nahuel Huapi, or Nahuel Huapi National Park, is a picture of serene beauty.**

Left and *below*: **The spectacular Perito Moreno Glacier is one of the few glaciers in the world that gets bigger each year.**

to the government, with the understanding that they would take care of it. From Moreno's generous gesture, the national parks system was born.

Terrain and climate vary from park to park and include subtropical forests, grasslands, cloud forests, marshlands, and savannas. Due to the varying environments, numerous birds, plants, and animals, ranging from the common to the endangered, are protected from harm in the national parks system. Several rare plants also grow in these areas, such as quebracho trees, candelabra cacti, and yatay palms.

From Falls to Glacial Wonders

The national parks hold many natural wonders within their borders. Iguazú Falls can be found in Parque Nacional Iguazú. This enormous waterfall, located on the Argentine/Brazilian border, welcomes thousands of eager sightseers every year. In Parque Nacional Glaciares, visitors can see glaciers that flow in from the ice fields. Huge ice chunks often break off the glaciers and crash into the water below, causing great waves of water to sweep out over the land. Parque Nacional Perito Moreno offers tourists a view of the Moreno glacier, which has had radical fits of movement throughout its history.

Polo

"Assassins" is what Argentine polo players are called by their rivals — and with good reason. These hard hitting, skilled players are regarded as some of the best in the world. Although the origins of polo are still disputed, the game was brought to Argentina by the British in the mid-1800s. Argentina was conducive to polo because of its expansive land, warm climate, and many horses, and the game quickly caught on. Soon, Argentine players had taken polo to a new international level.

The polo season begins in mid-September in Argentina. The game has four people on a team, and players try to hit the ball down a 295-yard (270-m) playing field to score a goal. A polo match is divided into periods called *chukkas*. Each chukka is seven-and-a-half minutes long, with six chukkas to a match. Players ride small, thoroughbred horses that are specially bred for this sport. These horses, called ponies, are noted for their strength and speed. The ponies are maintained by *petiseros* (pet-ee-SER-ohs), who train them rigorously. A polo pony will play in matches from the age of six to age ten. After that, it retires.

A RICH MAN'S SPORT

Throughout the world, polo is known as a rich man's sport. Polo ponies cost between U.S. $10,000 and U.S. $30,000, and players have to travel around the world to play in tournaments. Top players earn good money and are paid by team owners to play for foreign teams.

Below: Argentina has some of the best polo players in the world.

Raised for Sport and Money

Each polo player has many ponies that must be properly maintained. When top Argentine players join international teams abroad, their ponies are shipped to Europe for the season. When the season ends, the ponies are sold to the highest bidders. The players then return to Argentina to raise more ponies for the following season. Because polo ponies do not come cheap, money from their sale is a way for players to increase their earnings.

Above: **Ponies are specially bred for the game of polo. It costs a lot of money to raise these ponies, and top ponies fetch a high price on the market.**

Polo has become a family sport in Argentina. Fathers, brothers, and uncles from the same family might all play the game competitively. Children born into polo families are taught at an early age how to play the sport. They are given polo sticks when they are four or five years old and practice hitting balls as they ride around on their tricycles. As they get older and start playing competitively, they are given a numerical handicap, as in golf, to level the playing field. Handicapping ensures that one team does not have an unfair advantage over another.

Sheep

A Money Spinner

Argentina is one of the biggest wool producing countries in the world. The southern area of Mesopotamia, the southeastern pampas, the northwestern stretch of land that covers the Andes and reaches into Bolivia and Chile, and large portions of Patagonia rely on sheep farming to support their economies.

Patagonia is probably the most well-known sheep farming area in Argentina. Because the land is not fertile for farming cash crops and cannot be used for other industries, sheep farming has prospered there. The Patagonian provinces of Río Negro, Chubut, and Santa Cruz have become true assets in the sheep farming industry.

Several different types of sheep are found in Argentina. The Corriedale is a type of sheep that originally came from Scotland. It produces a high volume of wool, although the quality is not very good. The wool tends to be thick and rough — not as soft as wool from other sheep. Merino sheep produce less wool than

Below: **Sheep raised in Chubut province produce millions of tons of wool each year.**

Left: **A sheep is sheared for its wool, which will fetch a good price.**

Corriedales, but the wool is softer and, therefore, more expensive. Most sheep in Argentina are raised for their wool, although a small percentage are sold or killed for their meat. Some sheep are reared for their hides, although the demand for sheep hides is nowhere as high as that for fur skins or leather hides from cattle. Only a small fraction of all hides produced in Argentina come from sheep.

Every spring, sheep are sheared. Their fuzzy coats are collected and spun into wool, which is often sold to make clothes. Special workers visit estancias to do the shearing for the sheep farmers. These workers, who are called *comparsas* (com-PAR-sas), specialize in shearing sheep and are different from the regular ranch hands that work at the estancias all year long.

Sheep farmers have two assets in their business: their sheep and their land. They make a living selling wool to local and foreign clothing manufacturers. The value of the land is determined by the number of sheep that can graze a specified area. The greater the number of sheep that can graze the area, the more productive the land and the higher its corresponding worth.

The Tango

Argentina is well known for the sensual music and dance called the tango. Throughout the years, the tango's popularity has risen and declined, but, despite its low points, it always returns to favor and is danced with passion.

The tango has its roots in Buenos Aires, the capital of Argentina. During the nineteenth century, Buenos Aires was a melting pot of different ethnic groups and cultures. Groups of Europeans, Africans, and locals lived together in the same city and shared an important aspect of their respective cultures — music. Toward the end of the century, the mixing of these various music and dance styles gave way to what we now know as the tango. It was originally danced by people from the lower class and owed much of its success to the popularity it gained in brothels during the late 1800s. Because of its questionable beginnings, the tango was initially shunned by the more conservative upper class. Slowly, however, the dance made its way into more respectable social circles.

Below: **The tango is popular not only in Argentina but, increasingly, all over the world.**

64

In the twentieth century, the tango gained in appeal. More and more people began to enjoy the steps and sounds of the dance. When talented musicians began to play tango music, the appeal became even stronger, and when the dance became all the rage in Europe, the wealthy people of Argentina embraced it. Soon, recording companies joined in the growing tango craze and began to make records featuring tango musicians. Carlos Gardel is the most famous of these musicians.

The Tango Man

Carlos Gardel was a French immigrant who came to Buenos Aires at a young age. Fascinated by theater and music, Gardel got his big break in 1917 when he recorded the song "Mi Noche Triste" (My Sad Night). This song and his recording contract were the start of Gardel's success. He later performed all over the world and acted in seven films. His career, however, was cut short by a fatal plane crash in 1935. When Gardel's body was returned to Buenos Aires, it was met by thousands of fans who mourned the great singer's death.

Above: **Carlos Gardel is considered the tango's biggest star.**

THE BANDONEÓN

Several instruments, such as the guitar, flute, violin, and piano, give tango music its distinct sound. The *bandoneón* (ban-doe-nee-ON), however, is probably the most important instrument to the tango sound. It is a type of accordion that is difficult to play. Many of the first stars of tango music were bandoneón players. The instrument is no longer manufactured. Old bandoneóns are passed down in families from generation to generation.

Teatro Colón

The Teatro Colón is located in Buenos Aires, just off Avenida 9 de Julio, a central street in that city. Every year, the Colón attracts top singers from around the world. With the building's European design and the high caliber of performers who visit, the Colón has helped to maintain Buenos Aires' position as the "Paris of Latin America."

Teatro Colón opened in 1908 after many years of work. Plans for the building were initially drawn up in the late 1880s, and the architect had hoped the Colón would be finished within a few years. Construction, however, did not go according to plan. It took nearly twenty years and three architects to complete the building, thus, the Colón's eclectic mix of architectural styles. The exterior is mainly Greek in style, while the interior is a combination of German, French, and Italian Renaissance styles. Construction was finally finished in 1907, and the theater was opened to the public the following year.

Below: **The opera house Teatro Colón is one of the most elegant buildings in Argentina.**

A Sight to Behold

The Colón is a massive structure that occupies an entire city block in downtown Buenos Aires. The theater can hold 3,500 patrons and employs more than 1,300 people. Its auditorium is said to have among the best acoustics in the world. It is an astounding seven stories high and is decorated in red and gold. Patrons can sit on the main floor of the auditorium or in one of the six tiers of private boxes that encircle it. Performances take place on the huge revolving stage, which makes scene changes easier and faster. People can enjoy performances from April to December, which is the Colón's season for entertainment.

Above: **The interior of the opera house has been graced by numerous local and international artists who have enthralled its audiences.**

Attracting the Best

Teatro Colón is the perfect setting for the impressive artists who perform there. Ballet artist Mikhail Baryshnikov and opera stars Placido Domingo and Luciano Pavarotti are just a few of the famous artists who have performed there. In addition to opera, the theater also hosts concerts, recitals, and ballets. Teatro Colón is home to the National Symphony Orchestra and the National Ballet, making it a primary cultural center in Argentina.

Tierra del Fuego

Far to the south, past the Patagonian glaciers and the dangerous Strait of Magellan lies Tierra del Fuego, the "Land of Fire." This large island is found at the tip of South America and is divided between the countries of Argentina and Chile. The Argentine side is part of the Tierra del Fuego/Antártida/Las Islas del Atlántico Sur province. The capital of the province is Ushuaia, a city located on the southwest corner of Argentina's part of the island.

Tierra del Fuego is separated from Argentina's mainland by the Strait of Magellan. The island was once part of the mainland, but, thousands of years ago, water started to seep across the continent, eventually isolating the island from the rest of the country. The climate is subantarctic. Temperatures range from 24° F (-4° C) in the winter to 60° F (16° C) in the summer. Extreme temperatures are moderated by the ocean, making the weather slightly tolerable but cold nonetheless. Fierce winds sweep across the land from September through March, and severe weather is not unusual. The Andes Mountains, which run between Argentina and Chile on the mainland, continue on the island.

Below: **The city of Ushuaia was founded in 1884.**

Left and *below:*
**Ferdinand Magellan
and his ships rounded
Tierra del Fuego
during the voyage that
led to the founding of
a European settlement
on the island in 1520.**

Tierra del Fuego has been inhabited for the past 10,000 years. Four groups of indigenous people have lived there: the Onas, the Haus, the Yámanas, and the Alacaluf. All four groups became extinct when Europeans began living on the island. The first European to discover Tierra del Fuego was Ferdinand Magellan. In 1520, Magellan crossed the dangerous strait that was later named after him. After Magellan's discovery, many others came to explore the island. Today, the Argentine side of Tierra del Fuego has about seventy thousand inhabitants.

The Strait of Magellan is known for its high winds and treacherous waters. Several ships have been unable to pass through the strait, and many have sunk in its cold waters. Before the Panama Canal was built in 1914, ships used the Strait of Magellan to travel between Europe and the Pacific. Since then, the Strait has been used less often but is still a big shipping channel, especially for oil.

Tierra del Fuego was originally prosperous because of a successful sheep farming industry. Today, the island still has traditional estancias and sheep farmers, but the tourism and electronics industries have become more important to the economy. With a rugged terrain and a large national park on the island, there is a lot to explore for those willing to make the long trek to Tierra del Fuego.

Train to the Clouds

Seeing Argentina from High Above

In the northwestern region of Argentina is a city called Salta, which is located in the province of the same name and is the departure point for a truly spectacular ride. For those seeking adventure, *Tren a las Nubes* (Tren a las NEW-bes), or the Train to the Clouds, is an exciting way to see parts of Argentina.

The Train to the Clouds was a project that began in 1911, when a French engineer drew up plans for the railway. Ten years later, in 1921, construction began on this momentous undertaking. Richard Maury, an engineer from the United States, was in charge of building the railway, and he did an incredible job. Maury designed a zigzagged track that allowed the train to climb very steep inclines over relatively short distances. Construction of the railway was not completed until 1948, twenty-seven years after it was started. A lack of funds was blamed for long delays. The train, which is still in use, runs from Salta, Argentina, to Socompa, Chile. Passengers can ride the Train

Below: **The Train to the Clouds leaves Salta every Saturday and returns the same night.**

70

to the Clouds every Saturday, but it is necessary to schedule a trip far in advance, since the train runs only from April to November every year, and tickets sell out quickly.

Above: **Traveling on the Train to the Clouds is an awesome experience. A sense of adventure, a love of nature, or a desire to experience the unusual will keep the passenger interested throughout the journey.**

A Breathtaking Ride

Passengers on the Train to the Clouds are in for a real treat. The scenery is breathtaking, with Andes landscapes dominating the view. The entire train ride is a long 917 miles (1,475 km). At one point during the journey, the train climbs almost 10,000 feet (3,048 m) in just under 125 miles (201 km)!

The size and length of the railway become especially apparent when the train passes through twenty-one tunnels and crosses thirty-one bridges. There are thirteen viaducts, which are long, high bridges that span deep valleys. Perhaps the most amazing of these viaducts is La Polvorilla, which is supported by six enormous towers and rises to an extraordinary 13,780 feet (4,200 m). Crossing a viaduct provides passengers with an incredible view that extends far below them.

Yerba Mate

To Quench Thirst and More!

When Argentines get thirsty, they reach for an energizing drink called mate, which has been enjoyed throughout South America for hundreds of years. Also popular in Uruguay and Paraguay, mate is a drink with a kick. It contains about three times as much caffeine as a cup of coffee and is thus said to invigorate the drinker. People enjoy the taste of the herb and the energy boost it gives them. Mate is believed to have medicinal properties. It cures slight ailments, eases stomachaches, aids digestion, and boosts the immune system.

Yerba mate is a green herb grown in Paraguay and Mesopotamia. It was first cultivated by the Jesuit Missionaries of the area. It is part of the holly family of shrubs and grows in the shade of the subtropical rain forests. Yerba mate leaves look very similar to tea leaves. To prepare mate, you need a gourd, a bombilla, mate leaves, and hot water. People use hollowed out gourds, instead of cups or mugs, to drink mate. The gourds are round and small, just big enough to fit in your hand. Some fancier gourds are made of silver and have intricate designs. To make mate, the gourd is filled more than halfway with mate

Below: **The national drink of Argentina is made from the leaves of yerba mate trees.**

leaves dampened with cold water. After a few minutes, hot water is poured over the leaves until the gourd is filled to the brim. Usually, foam covers the top of the gourd. Depending on their preferences, people may add some sugar.

Bombilla — Not Your Regular Straw

After mate is prepared, a bombilla is used to drink it. A bombilla is a long straw that can be made either from cheap metal or from gold and silver. Instead of being a smooth pipe all the way up, a bombilla has a small, round globe at the end. This globe has little holes in it and acts as a strainer to catch all the herbal leaves. It lets the drinker enjoy the flavor of mate, without a mouth full of herbs! Mate is traditionally a communal drink, meaning the gourd is passed around from one person to another. Everyone uses the same bombilla to drink. When the gourd is empty, it is filled again with hot water and passed on to the next person.

RELATIONS WITH NORTH AMERICA

Argentina's relations with the United States and Canada have seen great improvement in the 1990s. Throughout most of the twentieth century, however, Argentina practiced a policy of isolationism, or avoiding close relationships with other countries. This policy was a huge disadvantage to Argentina. As other countries grew and prospered, it slipped economically. So, to keep the situation from getting worse, Argentina developed closer ties with two economically powerful countries — the United States and Canada. These two countries now enjoy greater trade with

Opposite: **U.S. President Bill Clinton visited Argentina on October 16, 1997. During his stay, he laid a wreath at the base of the monument to General José de San Martín, after which he was presented with a bouquet by a group of children.**

Argentina than before. They have also forged a more unified stand on human rights, freedom of speech, and other matters of mutual interest.

Most of the changes and improvements in Argentina's foreign policy can be credited to Argentine President Carlos Saúl Menem. When he took office in 1989, he vowed to make good foreign relations with the United States his number one priority. Judging from recent warm relations between the countries, President Menem seems to have achieved that goal.

Above: **On January 11, 1999, Bill and Hillary Clinton hosted a state dinner for Argentine President Carlos Menem.**

Early Relations

The history of relations between Argentina and the United States has not always been smooth-sailing. One country often ignored the other's position on important accords and treaties. These differences are only now being resolved.

Several factors contributed to Argentina's past conflict with the U.S. Argentina was a member of the Non-Aligned Movement (NAM), a group of nations, formed in 1955, that wanted to remain neutral in the Cold War, a period of nonviolent hostility between the United States and what was then the Union of Soviet Socialist Republics (U.S.S.R.). In 1982, Argentina's military government attacked the British-inhabited Falkland Islands, without declaring war. The British were the strongest ally of the United States at the time, so the attack greatly angered politicians in Washington, D.C.

Above: British soldiers were involved in a war with Argentina over the Falkland Islands in 1982, causing tension between Argentina and the United States, which had good relations with Britain.

Negative Actions

In the late 1970s and early 1980s, the United States accused Argentina of human rights violations on a number of occasions. Argentina, on the other hand, voted against some U.S. proposals in the United Nations and other organizations. These actions, and others, damaged Argentine-American relations. Because of the power and influence of the United States during this period, Argentina paid the penalty for its actions — the country was left behind, virtually becoming part of the third world.

A New Direction

Currently, Argentina's foreign policy has a new focus. President Menem has attached great value to democracy, human rights, and the economy. Menem has succeeded in overcoming the high inflation of his country, expanding trade with other nations, and increasing the production of goods for internal and external consumption. Argentina is now recognized as one of the most important emerging markets in the world.

In the early 1990s, Argentina provided forces for the Western Alliance, which included the United States, Britain, and France, to end the Gulf War. In 1994, it committed forces to end the crisis in Haiti by restoring the elected government. Both these actions were symbolic gestures of goodwill and cooperation by Argentina and were well-received by the United States.

Opposite: Argentina's open economy allows major U.S. food chains, such as McDonald's, to have a stake in the country's economy.

Trade with the United States

Argentina has enjoyed a 400 percent growth in U.S. investments since 1989. The United States is now Argentina's single largest investor. In 1997, Argentina exported a total of U.S. $25.4 billion worth of goods and imported some U.S. $30.3 billion from the rest of the world. It exported U.S. $2.3 billion to the United States directly and received U.S. $4.5 billion in imports from it, making the United States Argentina's second-largest trading partner after Brazil and giving both countries an important reason to continue their close relations.

Import and Export Markets

Food products make up a major share of Argentine exports. In fact, Argentina is the world's eighth-largest food producer and the fifth-largest exporter of food goods. There is also a large overseas market for Argentine fuels, fats and oils, meat, and machinery. Together, these markets consume nearly 40 percent

Below: **Besides yerba mate, another popular drink among Argentines is Coca Cola, a product of the United States.**

78

of Argentine exports. Machinery, electronic equipment, chemicals, plastics, and metals make up most of Argentina's imports.

Above: **Bill Clinton's visit to Argentina in 1997 was aimed at promoting U.S. economic ties in the region. On the last leg of a three-country South American tour, Clinton met Buenos Aires residents at a local market.**

Other Efforts: From Nato Ally . . .

In the late 1990s, Argentina became part of the military alliance of the United States. In 1997, it became a major additional NATO (North Atlantic Treaty Organization) ally, a position held by only seven other nations.

. . . to "War" Partner

Argentina's efforts to establish stronger economic and political ties with the United States bore fruit when U.S. President Bill Clinton visited the country in 1997 as part of his tour of South America. During his visit, Menem and Clinton agreed to declare war on common problems — drug trafficking and terrorism. The meeting, which received wide press coverage, was seen as a success for both countries.

Relations with Canada

In the past, Argentina and Canada had many things in common, such as their multicultural populations. They were politically stable and economically among the most prosperous countries in the world in the nineteenth century. Despite these similarities, however, they never prospered from their shared position. Each country developed on its own, and the two became competitors rather than partners.

Many of the factors that resulted in Argentina's problems with the United States also gave rise to poor Argentine-Canadian ties. Because Argentina's policy of isolationism did not allow Canada much room to capitalize on trade opportunities, Canada's foreign policy, to a great extent, did not include Argentina. Since President Menem took office, Canada has shown more interest in establishing strong ties with Argentina and in creating an economic partnership.

Above: **Canadian Prime Minister Jean Chrétien wants to increase trade between Argentina and Canada.**

Jean Chrétien's Role

Canadian Prime Minister Jean Chrétien visited Argentina twice in the 1990s. His first visit, in 1995, focused on trade between the two countries. Chrétien was accompanied by 250 business people who were interested in exploring the Argentine market. The meeting was a success, and what followed was a great wave of Canadian investments in Argentina.

Chrétien visited Argentina again in January 1998, with a group of people called *Team Canada*. Six hundred Canadians accompanied the prime minister, including business people, government officials, education representatives, and children. It was the greatest business mission in Argentina's history. By the year 2000, Canada plans to be Argentina's third-largest foreign investor, after the United States and Spain. This goal has endeared Canada to Argentina, and Menem is enthusiastic to continue their relationship.

Canada has already invested in Argentina's natural resources, such as oil and natural gas, and has expanded into mining. There are also other markets, such as forestry, industry, and telecommunications, that Canada is hoping to explore. With many large Canadian companies already located in Argentina, and many small and medium businesses keen to move there, Canada has a vested interest in the Argentine economy.

MERCOSUR

MERCOSUR, or the Common Market of the Southern Cone, is an agreement signed in 1991 to establish a free market in four South American countries: Argentina, Brazil, Uruguay, and Paraguay. MERCOSUR allows these countries to buy and sell goods from each other without paying the high tariffs they impose on other countries. The agreement is beneficial to all four countries because it increases their trade profits. Since MERCOSUR was established, Chile and Bolivia have been admitted as associate members.

Currently, Jean Chrétien is pushing to get Canada membership into this group. MERCOSUR represents 190 million people in South America and is, thus, a big market. President Menem has promised to help admit Canada into MERCOSUR. Although Canada has not yet been given membership into the group, negotiations have made some progress. In 1998, Canada became chair of the Free Trade Area of the Americas (FTAA), a position it will hold for eighteen months. FTAA is a free trade zone of the Americas, from Alaska to Tierra del Fuego, that thirty-four countries in the Western Hemisphere have agreed to set up by the year 2005.

Left: **Jean Chrétien and Carlos Menem met at the Casa Rosada Government House on the first day of Chrétien's official business visit to Argentina.**

Tourism

The tourism industry is alive and well in Argentina, with 4.5 million people visiting the country every year. Argentina is the most popular tourist destination for travelers to South America. Over the past ten years, the country's tourism industry has made impressive strides. The 1990s have seen an astounding 200 percent increase in tourist arrivals. There are over one hundred flights a week from major cities in the United States and Europe. Tourists who come from North America and Europe can enjoy two summers a year — if they time their vacations right.

Buenos Aires is the heart of Argentina, and no trip is complete without spending a few days in the capital. It is home to over six thousand restaurants, discotheques, cafés, and nightclubs, delighting even the most active of travelers. The city's museums, theaters, and dance halls provide tourists with cultural insight into Argentina's people and lifestyle. After visiting Buenos Aires, travelers can venture down the coast to

Below: **American tourists in Buenos Aires strike a pose with the pigeons that gather in a particular part of the city.**

Mar del Plata, an enormous beach resort. Here, tourists slather on suntan lotion and play in the surf. Hundreds of thousands of locals visit Mar del Plata every year. It is a great place to kick back and enjoy Argentina's long coastline.

Above: **American tourists on a boat ride enjoy Argentina's natural splendor.**

Adventure tourism is a growing industry in Argentina. It includes rafting, rappelling, kayaking, mountain bike riding, and other sports. Tourists can even go big game hunting in the pampas. Accommodations range from youth hostels to five-star hotels. The only problem is that travelers might not have the time to see everything the country has to offer.

Immigration

Immigration between Argentina and North America is so small that it is insignificant. In the past, the majority of immigrants to Argentina came from Europe, most notably Spain and Italy. Today, however, they come from other South American countries. Few Argentines seem to leave their country permanently for the United States or Canada. There are no major enclaves of Argentines living in large North American cities. *Enclaves* are distinct areas within a city or country that are inhabited only by people of another nationality or culture.

Made in Argentina

Argentina is the world's sixth-largest peanut producer, and, as of 1998, it is the world's largest peanut exporter, surpassing the United States and China. In the 1997–1998 period, Argentina produced 750,000 tons of peanuts and exported some 530,000 tons to countries around the world.

By the year 2000, Argentina will produce about 22 billion pounds of milk a year, about 50 percent more than what Argentines can consume at home. Because of cheap grazing conditions on the pampas, it costs Argentine farmers less than their U.S. counterparts to raise cows and produce milk. The United States is wary of Argentina targeting Mexico, a large importer of U.S. dairy products, as an export market. If all goes as predicted, the potential of the dairy industry will be a boon to the Argentine economy.

Madonna as Evita

Americans had a taste of Argentine culture when the movie *Evita* was released in 1997. With popular singer/actress Madonna in the lead role and heartthrob Antonio Banderas as her co-star, the film made over $50 million in the United States and $141 million

Above: **Madonna had the title role in** *Evita*, **a highly successful movie based on the life of Argentine icon Evita Perón. When a popular dance remix of the song, "Don't Cry for Me Argentina" was released in the United States, some time after the movie, it could be heard in the hottest clubs across the country.**

worldwide. It also spawned a soundtrack showcasing Madonna's vocal talents. The songs "You Must Love Me" and "Don't Cry For Me Argentina" were played regularly on the radio.

Kiss of the Spider Woman

Originally a book written by Manuel Puig, a famous Argentine writer, *Kiss of the Spider Woman* traces the lives of two inmates in a South American prison cell. In 1985, Puig's book was adapted into a movie, starring Hollywood stars William Hurt and Raul Julia. It was nominated for four Academy Awards in 1986. The book was also adapted into a wildly successful Broadway musical. The play originally starred singer/actress Chita Rivera in the role of the Spider Woman. She went on to win the Tony Award for Best Leading Actress in a Musical in 1993. The play won seven Tony Awards in all, including Best Musical. In 1995, *Kiss of the Spider Woman* went on a national tour of the United States. It was later revived on Broadway, with singer/actress Vanessa Williams taking over the part of the Spider Woman.

Left: **William Hurt won the Oscar for Best Actor in 1986 for his role in *Kiss of the Spider Woman*.**

ARGENTINA

BOLIVIA

PARAGUAY

Tropic of Capricorn

Humahuaca
Tilcara
JUJUY
San Salvador de Jujuy
Salta
SALTA
TUCUMÁN
San Miguel de Tucumán
CATAMARCA
SANTIAGO DEL ESTERO
CHACO
FORMOSA
Iguazú Falls
Iguazú
MISIONES
Corrientes

LA RIOJA
Santiago Del Estero
SANTA FE
CORRIENTES
MESOPOTAMIA

BRAZIL

SAN JUAN
Cosquin
Córdoba
Santa Fe
CÓRDOBA
ENTRE RÍOS

URUGUAY

PACIFIC OCEAN

Mount Aconcagua
(22,834 ft/6,960 m)

San Juan
Mendoza

CHILE

SAN LUIS

San Nicholás
San Antonio de Areco
BUENOS AIRES (FEDERAL DISTRICT)
La Plata
Río de la Plata

MENDOZA
Las Leñas
Santa Rosa
LA PAMPA
PAMPAS

BUENOS AIRES
Pinamar
Pinamar
Mar del Plata

Colorado
NEUQUÉN
Negro
Bahía Blanca

ATLANTIC OCEAN

RÍO NEGRO

Lake Nahuel Huapí
Bariloche

CHUBUT
Península Valdés
Chubut

ANDES

PATAGONIA

N

Comodoro Rivadavia

SANTA CRUZ

Mount Fitzroy
(11,073 ft/3,375 m)

Río Gallegos

FALKLAND ISLANDS
(ISLAS MALVINAS)

Strait of Magellan

Río Grande
TIERRA DEL FUEGO

Ushuaia
Beagle Channel

Legend
— Regional Boundary
■ Capital
● City
～ River

Above: The obelisk was built in 1936 to commemorate the 400th anniversary of the founding of Buenos Aires.

Andes B1–B4
Atlantic Ocean D3–D5

Bahía Blanca C3
Bariloche B3
Beagle Channel C5
Bolivia B1
Brazil D1–D2
Buenos Aires
    (Federal District) C2
Buenos Aires (province) C3

Catamarca B1
Chaco C1
Chile B1–B5
Chubut B4
Chubut River B4
Colorado River B3–C3
Commodoro Rivadavia B4
Córdoba C2
Córdoba (province) C2
Corrientes C1
Corrientes (province) C2
Cosquin C2

Entre Ríos C2

Falkland Islands C5
Formosa C1

Gran Chaco C1

Humahuaca B1

Iguazú Falls D1
Iguazú River D1

Jujuy B1

La Pampa B3–C3
La Plata C2
La Rioja B2
Lake Nahuel Huapi B3
Las Leñas B3

Mar del Plata C3
Mendoza B2
Mendoza (province)
    B2–B3
Mesopotamia C2–D1
Misiones D1
Mount Aconcagua B2
Mount Fitzroy B5

Negro River B3–C3
Neuquén B3

Pacific Ocean A1–A5
Pampas C2–C3
Paraguay C1
Paraná River C2
Patagonia B3–B5
Península Valdés C4
Pinamar C3

Río de la Plata C2
Río Gallegos B5
Río Grande B5

Salta B1
Salta (province) B1–C1
San Antonio de
    Areco C2
San Bernardo C3
San Juan B2
San Juan (province) B2
San Luis B2
San Miguel de Tucumán
    B1
San Nicholás C2
San Salvador de
    Jujuy B1

Santa Cruz B4–B5
Santa Fe (province) C2
Santa Fe C2
Santa Rosa C3
Santiago del Estero C1
Santiago del Estero
    (province) C1
Strait of Magellan B5

Tierra del Fuego B5–C5
Tilcara B1
Tucumán B1–C1

Uruguay D2
Uruguay River D1–D2
Ushuaia B5

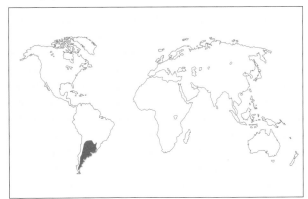

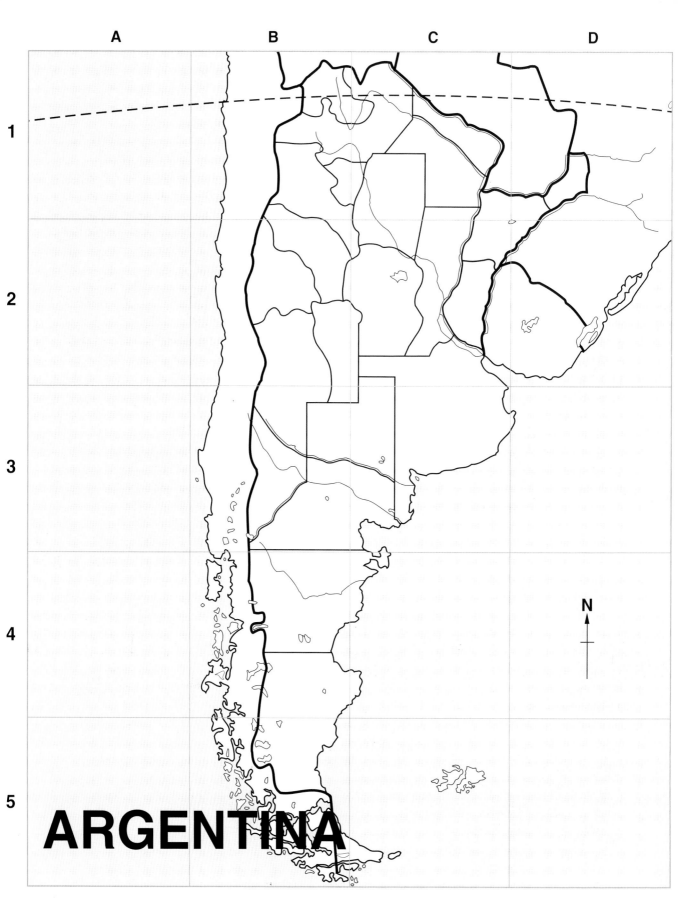

ARGENTINA

How Is Your Geography?

Learning to identify the main geographical areas and points of a country can be challenging. Although it may seem difficult at first to memorize the locations and spellings of major cities or the names of mountain ranges, rivers, deserts, lakes, and other prominent physical features, the end result of this effort can be very rewarding. Places you previously did not know existed will suddenly come to life when referred to in world news, whether in newspapers, television reports, or other books and reference sources. This knowledge will make you feel a bit closer to the rest of the world, with its fascinating variety of cultures and physical geography.

Used in a classroom setting, the instructor can make duplicates of this map using a copy machine. (PLEASE DO NOT WRITE IN THIS BOOK!) Students can then fill in any requested information on their individual map copies. Used one-on-one, the student can also make copies of the map on a copy machine and use them as a study tool. The student can practice identifying place names and geographical features on his or her own.

Above: **The pampas lie to the west of La Pampa province.**

Argentina at a Glance

Official Name	República Argentina, Argentine Republic
Capital	Buenos Aires
Official Language	Spanish
Population	36 million (1998 estimate)
Land Area	1,073,518 square miles (2,780,412 sq km)
Provinces	Buenos Aires, Catamarca, Chaco, Chubut, Córdoba, Corrientes, Entre Ríos, Federal District, Formosa, Jujuy, La Pampa, La Rioja, Mendoza, Misiones, Neuquén, Río Negro, Salta, San Juan, San Luis, Santa Cruz, Santa Fe, Santiago del Estero, Tierra del Fuego, Tucumán
Highest Point	Mount Aconcagua (22,834 feet / 6,960 m)
Longest River	Río de la Plata
Official Religion	Roman Catholicism
Current President	Carlos Saúl Menem
Famous Leaders	General José de San Martín — liberator; General Manuel Belgrano — served in the revolutionary army and created the national flag; Bernardino Rivadavia — first president of Argentine Republic; General Juan Perón — president from 1946–1955, and again from 1973–1974; Carlos Saúl Menem — president since 1989.
National Anthem	*Himno Nacional Argentino*
National Flower	*Flor de Ceibo* (Flower of the Ceibo Tree)
Important Festivals	Carnival, Feast of the Immaculate Conception, Festival de la Vendimia, the Gaucho Festival, National Folklore Festival.
Currency	Peso (P $1.00 = U.S. $1 as of 1999)

Opposite: **Art on the streets. Pencil sketches or portraits are done in less than an hour by the owner of this mobile store.**

Glossary

Spanish Vocabulary

asado (ah-SAH-do): the way meat is grilled over hot coals on a spit.

bandoneón (ban-doe-nee-ON): a type of accordion used in tango music.

boleadoras (bow-lee-a-DOOR-ahs): a weapon used by gauchos to capture animals.

bombachas (bom-BA-chas): loose riding pants worn by gauchos.

bombilla (bom-BEE-zha): a specially designed straw used to drink yerba mate.

cabildo (cah-BEEL-doe): a town council.

chorizos (cho-REE-sos): spicy sausages.

comparsas (com-PAR-sas): people who shear sheep for a living.

confitería (con-fit-a-REE-a): a café.

criollos (CREE-oh-yohs): people of European descent born in Latin America.

desaparecidos (des-a-par-eh-SEE-dos): the Argentine people who disappeared between 1976 and 1983, when the "Dirty War" took place.

empanadas (aym-pah-NAH-dahs): pastries stuffed with meat and vegetables, eaten as snacks.

ensalada mixta (en-sah-LAH-thuh MEEKS-ta): lettuce mixed with tomatoes, onions, oil, and vinegar.

estancias (es-TAN-see-uhs): large rural estates, such as cattle ranches and sheep farms.

fútbol (FOOT-ball): soccer; the favorite sport of Argentines.

La Virgen de Luján (lah VEER-hen day loo-HAAN): the patron saint of Argentina.

locro (LOH-kroh): a corn-based stew.

parrilla (par-REE-zah): meat grilled over hot coals.

petiseros (pet-ee-SER-ohs): people who maintain and train polo ponies.

poncho (PAWN-cho): a capelike coat worn by gauchos.

porteños (por-TAY-nyos): Argentines living in Buenos Aires or its suburbs.

quebracho (kay-BRA-cho): a tree with hard wood that grows in the Chaco region of Argentina.

Tren a las Nubes (Tren a las NEW-bes): "Train to the Clouds" that travels through the Andes from Salta, Argentina, to Socompa, Chile.

Vendimia (ven-dee-MEE-a): the annual festival held in Mendoza to celebrate the wine grape harvest.

yerba mate (YAIR-ba MAH-tay): a type of energizing, herbal tea enjoyed throughout Argentina and other parts of South America.

English Vocabulary

anti-Semitism: prejudice against Jews.

archipelago: a group of small islands.

asset: a skill or quality considered useful or valuable.

avant-garde: very modern art; artists or writers who introduce modern ideas.

capitalism: economic and social system in which individuals, not the state, own property and industry.

capybara: the largest rodent in the world.

demonstrations: gatherings of people who actively oppose something.

dialect: a certain, usually regional, form or sound of a language.

diversification: an increase (as a result of expansion) in the variety of goods produced.

epidemic: a widespread outbreak of sickness or disease.

expedition: a long journey with a specific purpose, such as exploration.

export: a product of one country sold in another country.

Falkland Islands: a group of islands off the eastern coast of Argentina that is held by Britain but claimed by both Argentina and Britain.

free market: an economy in which buyers and sellers decide on prices without government intervention.

gauchos: Argentine cowboys of the pampas.

gourd: a hard-shelled fruit that can be hollowed out as a cup or mug.

Great Depression: a period of world economic crisis that began with the stock market crash in 1929 and ended with the start of World War II.

handicapping: an advantage given to a player who is not very good at games, such as golf and polo, as a means of making the players more equal.

hydroelectric power: electricity produced by the energy of moving water.

indigenous: originating within a place, such as a country or geographic region.

inflation: an increase in the price of goods and services in a country.

intricate: detailed or complex.

isolationism: a government policy to severely limit interaction with other countries.

junta: a government that comes into power by military means rather than by elections.

Latin America: the countries of Central and South America, Mexico, and the West Indies.

mandatory: compulsory or required by law.

Nobel laureate: a person honored with the Nobel Prize, a prestigious award for his or her significant contributions to a particular field.

pampas: the grassy plains of central Argentina.

polo: a game between two teams of players on horseback who use wooden sticks to hit a ball for a goal.

proficiency: developed skill or ability.

socialism: an economic and social system in which a country's major industries are owned by the state.

South America: the fourth-largest continent in the world. South America includes the countries of Argentina, Bolivia, Brazil, Chile, Colombia, Ecuador, French Guiana, Guyana, Paraguay, Peru, Suriname, Uruguay, and Venezuela.

tango: a dance and musical form that has its origins in Argentina.

toucan: a South American bird with a big, colorful beak.

tumultuous: marked by disorder, confusion, agitation, or turmoil.

viaduct: a railway bridge over a valley.

More Books to Read

Andes Mountains. Wonders of the World series. Rose Blue and Corinne J. Naden (Raintree/Steck–Vaughn)

Argentina. Nick Caistor (Steck–Vaughn Library)

Argentina. Cultures of the World series. Ethel Caro Gofen (Times Editions)

Argentina. Enchantment of the World series. Martin Hintz (Children's Press)

Argentina. Festivals of the World series. Arlene Furlong (Gareth Stevens)

Argentina. Major World Nations series. Sol Liebowitz (Chelsea House)

Argentina: A Wild West Heritage. Discovering Our Heritage series. Marge Peterson and Rob Peterson (Dillon)

Argentina in Pictures. Visual Geography series. E. W. Egan, editor (Lerner)

Buenos Aires. Cities of the World series. Deborah Kent (Children's Press)

Cooking the South American Way. Easy Menu Ethnic Cookbooks series. Helga Parnell (Lerner)

The Tiniest Giants: Dinosaurs of Patagonia. Lowell Dingus and Luis M. Chiappe (Doubleday)

Videos

Living Edens: Patagonia. (PBS Home Video)

Social Studies: Folktales and Legends from Around the World. (The Humanities of Sciences)

Treasure of the Andes. (Educational Broadcasting Corp.)

Web Sites

www.surdelsur.com/indexingles.html

wfs.eun.org/schools/timeline/festivals/Argentina/index.htm

www.pbs.org/edens/patagonia/

www.odci.gov/cia/publications/factbook/ar.html

Due to the dynamic nature of the Internet, some web sites may stay current longer than others. To find additional web sites, use reliable search engines with one or more of the following key words to help locate information on Argentina: *Argentine history, Buenos Aires, gauchos, Ferdinand Magellan, Diego Maradona, polo, yerba mate.*

Index

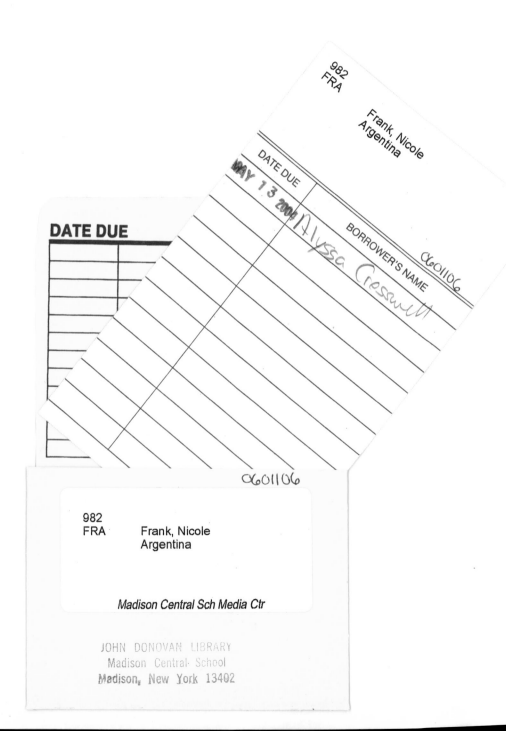

982
FRA   Frank, Nicole
           Argentina

982
FRA   Frank, Nicole
           Argentina

0601106

DATE DUE

MAY 13 2008   Alyssa Cresswell